One Step at a Time

written by

ANITA SAX

illustrated by

AIJA JASUNA

Printed in China
Production Location: G-Print International Inc.
Guangzhou, China
Date of Production: March, 2014
Cohort: Batch 1

Publishers Cataloging-in-Publication Data

Sax, Anita.
    One step at a time / written by Anita Sax ; illustrated by Aija Jasuna.
      p. cm.
    Summary: Roberta the Frog challenges her friend, Cesar the Caterpillar, to a race and advises him
to just take one step at a time.
    ISBN: 978-1-60131-152-8
    [1. Racing—Juvenile fiction. 2. Competition—Juvenile fiction. 3. Friends—
  Juvenile fiction.] I. Jasuna, Aija, ill. II. Title.

                                                          2013940348

115 Bluebill Drive
Savannah, GA 31419
United States

This book was published with the assistance of the helpful folks at DragonPencil.com

Roberta the Frog was quite the ambitious one. She could jump, leap, and hop better than anyone. Roberta was always ready for a challenge and loved to race. She was so fast that no one could ever keep up with her pace.

Cesar, on the other hand, wasn't so capable. He was an easy-going, slow moving caterpillar.

Cesar did not care to possess a competitive flair. Despite their differences, however, Roberta and Cesar were quite a pair.

One day, the two friends decided to go exploring through a rainforest where they had never been before. After a short time, hidden deep within many trees, they found an old abandoned structure. "What is that?" Roberta asked, looking up with curiosity. "It's a pyramid," replied Cesar, knowing this with certainty.

The pyramid looked like a gigantic triangle made of stone and had a long stairway that seemed to reach the sky.

Climbing the building
would be a real challenge,
and Roberta was eager
to give it a try.

"I'll race you," Roberta said, knowing this was the perfect opportunity to compete with her friend. Cesar's jaw dropped. He couldn't imagine even getting halfway up.

"I don't think I can!" he protested, overwhelmed at the thought. "Just take one step at a time," Roberta suggested, "and you'll do fine!"

Cesar swayed his furry head from
side to side. Although he wasn't very
convinced, Cesar decided to follow Roberta's
advice and put his worries aside. The two
friends took their positions at the bottom
of the first step. Cesar was feeling
like a complete wreck!

"Ready?" Roberta asked with excitement. Cesar wanted to say no, but Roberta didn't give him a chance to. "Get set!" she continued. "Goooo . . ."

Even before Cesar got a chance to
begin, it looked as though Roberta
was going to win. She was going
up each step so fast that the
race would surely not last.

"Come on, you slow poke!" Roberta hollered. "This race is so easy that winning will be a joke!"

Poor little Cesar let out a big sigh. He was frustrated knowing that Roberta had already left him far behind. Cesar felt like quitting, but he was not one to give up. No matter what, he was determined to reach the very top.

Meanwhile, Roberta was busy going faster and faster. There was no way of stopping her. She was eager to win the climb. Roberta was so confident that she was no longer taking one step at a time.

The thought of winning made her so happy that she started skipping two steps at once and then three. Cesar thought that Roberta was being unwise by not following her own advice. But Roberta didn't care, even though she wasn't being fair.

From time to time, she would look down at Cesar to make sure he was still far below. Roberta felt proud of herself and it showed. "This race is such a breeze," Roberta boasted, "that I could finish it with my eyes closed!"

Unfortunately, she was forgetting something. Roberta was no longer paying attention to what she was doing. Suddenly, just as she was taking her last leap to reach the top, Roberta didn't notice a slippery rock.

She stepped on top of it and lost her balance. Roberta had no chance. Before she could do anything, she slid. Roberta started tumbling quickly down the pyramid.

She tumbled to the right and tumbled to the left. All she could do was hold her breath!

No matter how hard she fought, Roberta couldn't bring herself to a stop! It hurt a lot!

As she bumped and thumped
against the steps, Roberta grumped.
She then moaned and groaned as her body
rolled. Before Roberta knew what
had happened, she was back down
where she had first started.

When all the dizziness went away, Roberta looked up. To her dismay, Cesar had reached the pyramid's very top! He had finished the climb and had won!

"How did you do that?" Roberta cried with complete disbelief.

"It was easy," hollered Cesar, happy to have first reached the finish line. "All I did was follow your advice and take one step at a time!"

The End